Learning Through Nature:
A manual for champion students

Madhusudan R. Damle

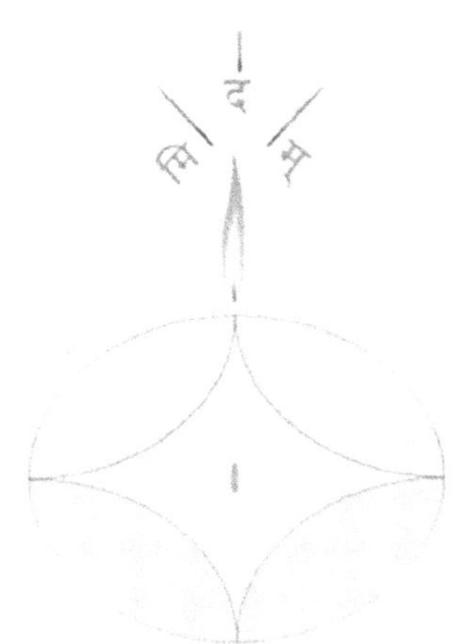

Learning Through Nature: A manual for champion students

by

Madhusudan R. Damle

Published by

Midam Charitable Trust

Midam Ashram

RS No. 144/5 Earikkarai Road

Kothapurinatham Village,

Puducherry- 605102

E-mail: midamashram@gmail.com
Web: www.midamashram.org
Phone: +91 9751076593

Type Setting and Layout

PAGE VIEW Book Designers

ISBN Number: 978-81-955254-0-9

ACKNOWLEDGEMENT

I express my gratitude to my father, Late. Shri. Raghunath Vishnu Damle,

Controller & three time winner of Ashoka Pillar Trophy,

Brook Bond India, Pvt.Ltd.

&

to my mother Late. Smt. Indirabai Raghunath Damle,

my first teacher who introduced me to mother nature.

CONTENTS

FOREWORD

I had the good fortune of meeting Respected Shri. Madhusudan R. Damle ji, first time, in the year 2009 at Pondicherry. I found the amazing ability to distill ancient spiritual truths into contemporary usable and practical guide lines in him. He conveyed "I can not tell you any spiritual truth that deep within, you don't know already. All that; I can do; is remind you of what you have forgotten." I liked Chapters 11 and 19 of this book, more.

With intense and compelling clarity, Shri. Damle ji's guidance holds the promise of leading us to our own best and highest place within, to resonate with and reflect the energy of true transformation. He makes enlightenment seem attainable and necessary for both individual peace and the health of our nation.

Regardless of one's religious or spiritual beliefs, his words of wisdom are ones that all should have exposure to. This book is best read; perhaps a chapter a day; to enable one to reflect upon the words and experience the truth of what has been read. Shri. Damle ji holds your hand like a guardian angel and takes you step - by - step towards leading a life.

The author has made the spiritual guidance accessible to everyone; writing it in a narrative form as conversation between a teacher and his students. The author uses words to guide readers beyond words.

I have searched for meaning of power, energy, success & life; but unfortunately I was searching outside myself. This book has shown me how to find life's elusive treasure within. This is a most extraordinary book to emerge in modern times - one that may well augur an evolutionary change in human consciousness. Read it, but not with your mind. Allow its mystic aroma to touch your innermost being!

Every time, I return to a segment of this book, I am surprised to find a new deeper meaning than the previous read. I heartily recommend this profoundly inspiring book to all seekers today. Truly an exceptional book that promises to make a real difference in people's; especially students' lives; by one of the most inspiring teachers on the subject.

If I have a spiritual guide, it is probably this book. Read it. It just might change your life. The author conveys a single profound message with timeless clarity of the ancient spiritual masters - There is a way out of human suffering by opening ourselves to the transforming experience.

If I were allotted only one book, I would choose this. Why? Because this book emanates a spirit of love and nation building; not only through its words, but in the spaces between the words. No book has touched me, nor embraced me as this one has.

It is more than just a book. It's a companion for a life time. The other books were appropriate for the twentieth century. This is for the twenty first!

At the end, I would like to add the conversation.

The student asks the question to the teacher - 'How will I know, when I have become a champion and useful in nation building'?

The teacher answers - "When you no longer need to ask the question!"

My best wishes!

- Dr. Krishnabhushan E. Mahashabde

Dr. K. E. Mahashabde completed his higher studies in Japan and is a renowned consultant architect, arbitrator & academician. He is the first doctorate holder in 3 different disciplines in India. Viz. Environmental Science, Urban Planning / Architecture and Law.

He is also the first architect in India holding a Ph. D. in Law and has served as a consultant architect to various departments of State and Central Govt., Municipal Corporation for various projects. He is also a former Principal of College of Architecture in Mumbai, former President, Architects & Engineers Association, Nashik and former President, Rotary Club of Nasik West.

AUTHOR'S NOTE

My dear students, I am sure everybody wants to become a champion in his or her life in their own chosen faculty. When we talk about becoming a champion, mastering the subject taught in school is what comes to the mind of a student, at first. But let me tell you that mastery of certain basic skills, which you are going to see in the subsequent chapters of this book, is not restricted to the academic syllabus of a school or college. Skills once acquired make a strong base for the students in any faculty they are interested in, for example games, drama, dance, debate, music, art, literature etc. But overall development is achievable; only when there is a strong personality at the base.

You are well aware of the commonly used phrase "A strong mind in a strong body". In this context, there are few more important aspects like emotions, lust, hate, fear, anger, undue attachments, ego and many likes and dislikes which we will be looking at in this book. A student is always in a cage of one or more of the above said cages, and he/she is trapped similar to a robot controlled by these traits, because of which he/she can't develop.

One can't develop one's personality in the complete sense; as these negative traits hinder the proper growth and development of one's personality. All of us want to come out of this cage and fly like a free bird.

The principles; we are going to study & practice will give us a freedom from the cage. At the end of this course, each one of you will feel free & more confident to walk on the road towards success. This course is beneficial for every student irrespective of caste, creed, religion or even nationality. It will awaken the global perspective in every reader. The world is becoming smaller and nowadays distance is no more a limitation because anything happening anywhere in the world, is known globally within no time.

Today's students are not only regional students but also global students and they are exposed to the world. All of us at Midam Trust, trust that you will follow this course practically and get benefited from it.

Our course will not only make students happy, but also make their parents, relatives, teachers and all those; who come in contact with them happy!

"My BEST WISHES TO YOU ALL!"

Madhusudan R. Damle
Founder & Director;
Midam Charitable Trust & KVM Research Laboratories,
Puducherry.

INTRODUCTION

My dear students, welcome to this special class of personality development! Each one of you want to be a champion student. First of all, you should believe that you already have a champion in you. But How? It is a well-known fact that all human beings possess an original capacity to become a champion in any faculty. Every human being is evolving and attaining that perfection in his or her life. We see this fact from our history and even in the present time, where we see both men & women excelling in many faculties. Both are warriors, scholars, artists, poets, writers etc. and the physical, mental & emotional excellence has been achieved by them.

Now, if we study their life achievements, we come to know that they have mastered certain traits and gotten over the shortcomings in their personalities. We read about these great personalities but forget to learn from them and we continue to live with our own shortcomings. And because, we let these few very important aspects go, we allow the shortcomings in us to hinder our growth.

We all like outings and hence I have decided to take you to different places to learn; instead of learning in the classroom and these different places and different topics will be interesting and you can grasp the subject at ease. We will observe our hurdles first, attend to them & then by removing those hurdles, we will march on the path of success gradually.

You must be wondering "How to do it?" The answer is "Just by doing it"!

We are going to study a dialogue between students and an experienced teacher; who has mastered his own personality. Out of curiosity, the students ask many questions. But we see the teacher answering all the deep life questions with love and patience through his practical experience. At the end of the journey, every student will be more confident while embarking on his or her every endeavour.

Every human being experiences challenges in his life. He is always struggling with one problem or the other. There are multiple problems in nature. To name the main, the problems could be physical, emotional, mental and philosophical. Many a times, it is seen that these problems are mixed and confusing. One does not know how to deal with them and which problem should be tackled first; if one goes ahead to deal with all of them at a time; then he finds a mixture of multiple problems as if all are acting together and finds no way to deal with them and then gets totally depressed and surrenders to them and becomes inactive.

It is seen that even after an individual's success in career, one carries few weaknesses and gets stuck again because of them and yet continues to carry them on. This takes away the individual's prime goal of bliss & makes one get caught in the cycle of happiness and sadness.

To overcome sadness or depression, one gets engaged in outward solutions; like visiting some entertainment programme or places of natural beauty, hill stations, rivers, seaside or even some pilgrimage places.

During these changes; he finds and experiences the sense of well-being but comes back to the same status after some days.

And he is always in search of a permanent solution to find peace and permanent delight in life.

The whole of life seems like a constant war with our physical, emotional, mental and philosophical hurdles and one gets caught & experiences that he remains constantly in a cage and then slowly becomes a robot controlled by these hurdles and the individual's growth remains stagnant. In the coming chapters, we are going to learn and practice the ways to become blissful and make all around us happy and blissful.

There is a dialogue between a teacher and his students; which can give us a formula of 'Right Mental Attitude' (RMA) towards dealing with problems.

Thirty children enrolled for a personality development workshop organized by their school, right towards the end of their term. All were eager to attend the workshop as the teacher; who was going to conduct it was a renowned professor; who had trained many eminent students; who are established in various disciplines. He; also; had a reputation of transforming his students into champions through his very practical and unique approach that encouraged his students to think independently and identify their hidden talents.

The first day of the workshop is about to begin. So without further delay, let us also join the students on Day 1.

Chapter 1: Frog: *What is fun to you is death to us!*

CHAPTER 1

Dealing with conflicts of the Mind

The venue for the workshop is the school classroom. All the students assembled in the classroom and took their respective seats. Soon the teacher arrived and all the children greeted the teacher with a good morning. After greeting the students, without wasting any time, the teacher immediately began with a question:-

Teacher: "What to do or What not to do?" My dear children; when such a situation comes; when you can't understand the problem, you should contact your parents, teachers, elders or your best friend and seek help. Instead of remaining in a confused state of mind, you should not hesitate to ask somebody. My dear students; many a times; our minds are crowded with conflicting thoughts, conflicts, contradictions, antagonistic thoughts creating confusions and fears of different kinds which may not be real in their true sense but imaginary and we become exhausted and feel weak because of them.

In such a mental condition; either aimless fights take birth or we prefer to give up and accept defeat.

Student: Sir, I have a question. What should we do at such times? Should we accept conflicts or accept defeat and prefer non acting or inaction?

Teacher: The simple thing at such times is to consult an elder, teacher, mother, father, brother, sister or friend & take their advice. Yes, this is actually a very simple and assured way of coming out of a depressing situation. It is important to open yourself completely & seek for an advice. Do not remain alone in that situation as it can lead to destruction of your personality.

Coming back to what I was saying; have you observed- "when do fights occur"?

Most fights take place when a selfish thought occurs or when demands are not legitimate. Right from childhood; we should learn to share food, toys etc. with our brothers, sisters and friends. A selfish mentality cannot be satisfied. It makes a person think, "I want more & more" to the extent that the individual feels that he/she should have everything and all others must remain deprived of even normal needs to sustain their lives. This leads to a sort of chaos and ultimately nobody remains happy in the society. If everyone is happy; we, all, shall be happy. Isn't it?

Student: Sir, what about the playful fights; that we have with friends and our brothers/ sisters?

Teacher: Children, a sour and sweet tease is a tonic for all. Normal teasing & jokes should be taken in sportsman's spirit. We can have fun but we must see to it that it should not cause physical or emotional hurt to anybody.

There's a story; in which; some children were playing near the bank of a river. While playing; they found that a frog was jumping around and it was a fun moment for all. But then, they got excited; while enjoying and in their excitement; they started throwing pebbles at the frog to make it jump higher.

Student: Sir, what is wrong in that?

Teacher: Well, fun is ok to some extent; but the frog got hurt and was bleeding and even then; they did not stop. The frog then cried and said " What is fun to you; is death to us!" What is the message here? The gist?

This story teaches us that it is okay to have fun; only to the extent that; nobody is hurt. Fun is good; when you tease someone in a friendly mood and jovial manner; When it goes beyond this and causes hurt, it is bad.

Sometimes, both boys and girls experience that someone is touching or pinching them abnormally in a manner which brings discomfort to them. At such times; they should take this problem to teachers, parents or trusted elders. They should never suffer this sort of discomfort and must seek help immediately.

Chapter 1: Points to Remember

1. *When there's a conflict in the mind- 'to do or not to do', remain quiet first and then ask a trustworthy person without hesitation.*

2. *Our demands should always be legitimate.*

3. *Try to remain happy and make others happy.*

4. *An occasional and light hearted prank for fun is okay; but it should not hurt anybody physically or emotionally.*

Chapter 2: Part 1

The Right Mental Attitude (R.M.A)

Today, the teacher took the students on a stroll outside the usual atmosphere of the classroom. As they walked on the broad pavement, beside the highway, he encouraged his students to ask their questions. One student who was already having a question in mind, immediately seized the opportunity and asked the following question:-

Student: Sir, at times; I feel so stagnant and upset that I don't know what I should do. What should be done at such times?

Teacher: At such times, the first and foremost thing is that you should try to remain calm. Just stop thinking and calculating on the pros and cons. Understand your problem and then approach the person you feel best for seeking an advice.

At that time; you keep the problem before the person, you reach out to and do not make contradictory statements based on preliminary calculations of your mind that is crowded with thoughts.

Student: But how to do that, Sir? I mean, my mind is confused and I feel that I must discuss all the confusions and seek answers from the advisor. No?

Teacher: That's fine; but when you go to the advisor, instead of having a discussion; you can just surrender and wait for receiving his/ her guidance to your problem.

Student: Oh! Doesn't that mean surrendering? What remains of me under the advisor's mercy? This is my failure then, isn't it?

Teacher: No, No! It is not that surrender; that is done in a battlefield; where one army surrenders to the other and the surrendered soldiers then accept whatever punishment that comes to them; such as prison, torture or even death.

Student: This seems like that only, Sir. How can it be different?

Teacher: This is what you have to understand. Here, surrender means you should just drop down the weapons of your contradictory arguments and just keep aside these FAQs and the force of arguments; as your queries and curiosity in times of confusion have a bias of ignorance.

Chapter 2.1: *Ask for guidance when you need help and listen attentively.*

This will then not be a surrender of the kind that you are thinking. But will be a preparation for you to listen to the the advisor with a calm approach so that you can find correct solutions. It is not a surrender for lifetime but surrender for getting a solution without any agitation and this is RMA Key for every student.

Student: What is this RMA, Sir?

Teacher: RMA stands for Right Mental Attitude. It is very important to be a seeker with this attitude and understand with a clear mind.

Student: Sir, I understand that this type of surrender is not like the surrendering of a soldier to an enemy which ultimately leads to death. But Sir, death is also a fact and many individuals have suicidal tendency and sometimes in depression commit suicide. How should one deal with death and then the question of what after death?

Teacher: Oh; my dear child; death is a relative truth of life!

Student: Means, is it the true end of everything?

Teacher: No, no. Do not jump to the end. It is never an end. See there are three conditions in life. You take birth which is the 1st stage, then you become a youth after crossing childhood. This is the 2nd stage. And then; there is the 3rd stage; where you become old.

Do you mean to state that childhood dies when you approach the stage of youth and when you approach old stage does the youthfulness inside die?

Student: Sir; it is confusing. I am not able to understand anything

Teacher: Okay. See you can't remain in the stage of childhood forever. In life; you grow and then become old and this is a natural phenomenon. As a child; you have to study many many subjects and while experiencing life, you should keep on practicing to make yourself perfect and then only; can you become a knowledgeable young person and join some faculty to do the best and grow your family, society, your nation and become a universal personality. And when you become old; you need not work physically but you can impart to others the great experience of life that you have. This is how in every faculty you have masters to teach and guide you in different faculties such as the teaching profession, sports, research, administration and more.

All these life's stages teach us that the physical form and duties change but the person remains the same within and passing onto the next stage is not death.

Student: But; ultimately one dies, no? Then death is sure. I understand the three forms child, youth and old age. But then what is death? What happens after death?

Teacher: What we identify as the body or form dies but there is a soul inside the body. It also experiences all that and it takes another form and grows further so there may be an end in some form; but it takes another form. Just like the 3 stages are not death; but a form of growth; similarly the death of the physical form is not death; but a change; where the energy; which we call as soul, gets transformed or born as another form. So; there is no death or extinction but changing of forms. Energy remains in the form of soul.

Students: Apparently ok. But then what ?

Teacher: "Then what ?" Please don't focus on death. Be in day tight compartments. Today is your day, which will be past tomorrow. Today is your day and it will create your tomorrow.

Student: Yes, Sir! Now I will concentrate only on my present duty and shall focus on my daily performance.

Teacher: Dear students, we always hear about morals, is it not? Do you know; what is your moral duty?

Student: Yes, Sir! We have heard and read many a times about morals and moral duties. But I do not know what is my moral duty as a student. Also; what will it be when I grow up and become independent.

Teacher: You have asked the right questions. We do not know our moral duty and hence have no idea how to fulfil the same.

See, it starts from our home only. What is your moral duty today? To exercise; your moral duty, you should be helpful to your brothers and sisters in performing their duties; like helping them in getting ready to go to school. Instead of only teasing all the time, you should help them in studies, games and other extracurricular activities; like dance, drama, homework etc.

You must start from small actions that help your parents. Doing your own study and not troubling them will also be an act of upholding your moral duty. Be on the side of righteousness and truth; as only truth prevails. It is permanent.

Student: Sir, what if standing by the truth clashes with our duty?

Teacher: How can this be? Our first and foremost duty is truth only and it can't clash or change with anything. This is only a mental assertion/ supposition.

Student: But how can we decide?

Teacher: See, whatever helps you grow in the light of truth is what you should decide to do. Your first occupation is to grow your personality. Aim high, study, keep good health, eat proper food and exercise. Help your family in the true sense and not for showing to others that you are helping.

When you follow all of these sincerely, how will truth clash with your duty?

Student: Oh! Now I understand. Sincerity in performing daily duty is my moral duty and also the truth. Thanks Sir!

Teacher: What happens; always with all of us; is that even before performing our duty, we start thinking of rewards and fulfilling petty expectations and these expectations hinder us and prevent us from doing proper actions and hence the real duty of the moment remains unattended leaving the result incomplete. But when you concentrate upon performing your duty without expectation, you can give 100 % of your abilities and reach the target. Remember, you must always concentrate on the task before you.

Student: Sir, you said to always be on the side of the truth. Can we not lie sometimes?

Teacher: It's a very good question indeed! See, my child; we always like to have fun. For fun, we at times lie initially and then disclose it later on but if these funny pranks cause physical or emotional damage or hurt to others, it is not good. As we learnt in the last lesson of the story of a frog.

Let us look at a situation. If a thief enters your house with a knife or a stick and asks you where your father has kept money? Knowing that he has already robbed you of a few possessions, will you truthfully show him where your father has kept all the money that he has earned by working hard for the family? Or, would you lie by saying that your father has kept all money in the bank?

Likewise, if a criminal is running after somebody with a knife and asks you to tell him which road 'X' has gone, so he can follow and kill him, what will you do? Will you tell a lie and show him the exactly opposite direction or would you tell the truth and put a person's life in danger?

At these times, such things may be lies on one level but they are not lies as they are not destroying anything or anyone but saving a family or a life- which is the ultimate truth.

But; you should recognize that such incidences are rare and hence; you should always take the path of the truth; as it will build positivity in you and help you grow into a universal personality.

Teacher: Alright Students, we have reached our playground. I am sure; you all have enjoyed the journey till here.

Student: Sir, what a surprise! We never thought of visiting the playground.

Teacher: Yes. See, if I would have told you earlier that after the highway walk; we shall be visiting the playground, then you would not have concentrated on our today's subject. Instead you would have imagined the ground and games; you like the most. Am I right ?

Student: Yes Sir; 100%! And I would have regretted later on for missing these important points that you shared with us.

Teacher: Hmm! Now, you should learn that even while doing little things; you should keep up concentration without expecting any specific outcomes or rewards in return for doing it. Do not think of it as a small act or calculate what you are going to get out of it. Small acts also can be of great help. You must have heard the saying – *"Take care of the pennies and the pounds will take care of themselves"*. Even while spending a single rupee, you should ask yourself – "Am I making proper use of it?" And ultimately; you will be in a position; where you can spend for a required thing at the right time. Take care while doing small actions and perform them with sincerity and perfection knowing that you are making a strong foundation for bigger things to happen.

Chapter 2, Part 1: Points to Remember

1. *When you are asking for help from somebody, first listen attentively, try to understand and then resolve.*

2. *Surrendering to a guide is not a lifelong surrender. It is done to get a solution and so there is no need for agitation.*

3. *Understand this to be the RMA key (Right Mental Attitude) for getting any solution.*

4. *Death is but a birth for another form.*

5 *The moral duty of the student is to study, take care of health and also to help friends and family a little.*

6 *Perform duty of the day and do not work for rewards.*

CHAPTER 2: Part 2

Freeing the mind from the trap of expectations

The students returned to their classroom after having fun in the playground. As they settled in their respective seats, the teacher asked them to recollect what they had learnt in the playground. One student promptly summarized: -

Student: In our last session, you had concluded that small actions can lead to something big. Sir, can you explain with an example; how small small works become big?

Teacher: Well recollected! Just see, every day; we leave for school in the morning at around 7 to 7.30 a.m. On our way, sometimes; we see that some construction work is going on and a worker is busy in laying small bricks with the help of cement and sand, arranging the bricks one on top of the other. You just ignore it and move forward but when you come back home by 4 or 5 p.m., you are astonished and surprised to see a big wall has taken a form and you can't see the view beyond it, that you saw in the morning.

Student: Yes, Sir! I have noticed this many times in my city. In front of my house; there was no road and it was difficult for us to walk. Once in our vacation; I went over to my relatives; came back after 15 days and saw a very big metal road. I was very happy.

Teacher: In the same way, we grow in our personality by learning the small small things and attending to the tasks with care and concentration. By dealing with many subjects and facing many situations; we become more and more confident.

When we see people with bigger responsibilities in high positions, we understand that they have to take big decisions and they take it with a calm mind, irrespective of any fear or worries about consequences. They focus on their tasks in hand with a calm mind, taking decisions after weighing in all the pros and cons and then they complete the task.

A person who has a balanced mind is calm at all times and in all situations. He does not get excited with success or depressed with failure. He is not under the influence of fear or anger and he can be considered to be a true champion; who performs his actions with perfection.

Student: Teacher, please give us some examples that are just perfectly suitable for us.

Teacher: Sure, my dear child! When you are taking part in a drama, a debate or an oration. Please, do not think about any failure! Just perform quietly with concentration

Chapter 2.2 *If you play sincerely and take joy in the game, you will experience a happiness that is beyond success or failure.*

and ease. And when you do that, you perform well. But if you have doubts and fear, you will forget to speak or act even if; you have prepared perfectly well.

Student: Yes, Sir. That is ok. If we approach this way, we may not be 100 % perfect but at least; we shall not fail in our task; while performing it. We can always prepare better for the next time.

Teacher: What are competitions for?

Student: To be a winner, Sir.

Teacher: Can you play without thinking of only winning?

Student: No Sir. We have to play to only win in a competition.

Teacher: In that case, you will either win and become happy or if you fail, you will become sad and nervous, right?

… But, if you play perfectly as per rules and regulations of the game and take joy in that game, you will have something more than loosing or winning. You will experience a bliss which is experienced beyond victory or failure. So; irrespective of whether you win or lose, you will be a happy player. See; you cannot decide to either win or loose. This takes out the real spirit from you. Nothing is in your hand always; as so many factors decide the outcome. You may or may not win.

But, you can decide to play your best with full focus and vigour, without thinking of any result. So; in this *'conditioned mind'* you will remain happy and satisfied that you have given your 100 %.

This will always keep you on the right path of doing your task; unattached with any sort of success or failure.

See; success may bring you confidence or failure may bring distress. But; both are mere emotions; which have the potential of causing great hindrance in your growing into a good personality. You have to attain a serene quietude; where; there is no excess rejoicing, no anger or fear and this condition is attained by many great personalities; who have come out of the trap of petty emotions.

Chapter 2: Part 2: Points to remember

1. *A balanced mind is calm at all times and is not excited with success or depressed with failure.*

2. *A true champion is not under the influence of anger or fear and performs all actions with perfection.*

3. *If you play sincerely and take joy in the game, you will experience a happiness that is beyond success or failure.*

CHAPTER 3

Listening to the inner voice

The students assembled outdoors; adjacent to the ground and looked towards their teacher, both curious and eager to grasp the topic of today's discussion. The teacher pointed towards a bullock cart; that was moving towards the end of the ground and spoke:-

Teacher: Boys, can you see a bullock cart at the end of this ground?

Student: Yes, Sir.

Teacher: Who is driving it?

Student: The cart-driver, Sir.

Teacher: Yes. But observe that the cart driver is directing the bullock with nudges and as long as the bullock follows the instructions of the driver, it keeps walking in the right direction.

Similarly, if we listen to our inner driving force or our inner voice, we will be on the right path and we shall progress joyfully, on the path of the truth.

Student: Sir, that's ok; but many a times; we feel like being inactive and lazy and feel like doing no action.

Teacher: It is always better; if we remain in action and in fact one cannot remain inactive any time as we have learnt that "You do it or you will be forced to do it ".

See that; activity is always going on. Even when you eat or sleep. You feel nothing when you are sleeping, but the action of digestion and assimilation is going on even without your direct action. Even when you are standing, breathing is going on continuously without your noticing it.

All our 5 senses are at work at all times. You are at work all the times. Even if; you are only thinking and simply standing near a window, your eyes catch images from the outside. If you stop thinking and observe closely you can see all the fine details, your nose makes you understand the fragrance of flowers from the window itself, your ears can hear the chirping of the birds. While standing, if you just eat sweets; your tongue tells you that you are eating a sweet. Suddenly; if an insect bites you, your hand shakes and twitches instantly and the insect flies off.

Chapter 3: *Be conscious of your inner guide.*

So, one cannot say that one is inactive at any given time. But, what I want to say is that by the help of these senses, you must do a right action. And it is here that the mind comes in play. It makes you act.

But, doing any act is not sufficient. The action should be directed by discriminative intelligence and this makes you a better human being. Doing right action is necessary. We must know that action gives us experience and strength.

Student: That's fine. But how can we listen to the inner voice, Sir?

Teacher: You know it, my friend. If you eat more, your stomach gets upset. This is a physical experience. If you tell a lie, you may feel bad for some time; as your inner voice tells you that you lied. It pricks you. If you correct yourself and keep away from it, you get confidence.

Student: How can we differentiate between discriminative intelligence, mind and senses?

Teacher: The senses are always in demand. The tongue wants taste, eyes want videos, ears want to listen to music and skin wants the touch of something which gives you a good feeling.

These are the emotional expectations of senses. Sometimes the mind accepts these feelings and one goes after them. But the discriminative intelligence tells you what is good and bad for you. It is said - let the mind go; but not the physical. This is-what is called the inner voice, which can take you ahead towards what is right, towards that which is good; not only for you but for all around you.

Chapter 3: Points to remember

1. Be conscious of your inner guide.

2. Make use of your senses with awareness.

3. Do good which is good for others too.

Chapter 4: *Do not think of any inferiority in yourself or others.*

CHAPTER 4

A universal power available to all human beings

The venue for today's lesson was the same ground, where the children had assembled previously. Only the time of the session was different; as it was nearing sunset. The students were quite curious; as to what they were going to learn today. The teacher started the day's lesson:-

Teacher:　See friends, there are infinite qualities inside of humans. We know this, when we read life stories of the many masters in many fields.

Even; an uneducated individual, so called by the public in general, because of his lacking basic academic degrees can write great poetry, become a big businessman, hold great positions in sport and art. If you observe the lives of such persons, you can understand why they became great. It is because they utilised their dormant qualities. On the other hand, some; so called educated individuals; take to different vices and ruin their beautiful lives. This is simply because they do not use the dormant qualities inside of them. Many people; who do not have basic senses; like seeing or hearing or are having some or the other form of disability, can with their effort; progress more than individuals; without any disability.

Student:　Sir, how can be identify these qualities?

Teacher:　Look, I have brought you to this ground and it is the time of sunset. Just look up above, in the sky. Watching the marvellous scenery of the sky makes you feel a deep silence, isn't it? Watching the shining stars, some clouds in between and suddenly, when the moon shedding its milky light on to the earth, comes into sight, it brings a calmness in your whole being, isn't it?

You see; a great energy is at work there. As we are also a part of the universe; we also possess that energy. Nature looks beautiful; as it is pure and has no anger, greed, lust etc. It enjoys the fullness of the universal energy.

Student:　Why can't we also enjoy the fullness of nature?

Teacher:　But; we human; beings can't experience this; as our whole energy is covered by our petty vices, demands, lust, anger. All our senses are craving for their demands and hence; the true energy is unused because of these demands.

And; when the number of such human beings increases; even the natural resources available to all of us; come in danger.

We do not realize what is given to us as an individual; but we destroy the wealth available outside us in the form of nature. Humans destroy the flora and fauna and add to the human miseries.

But, all are not like that. A few sense the master inside them and act according to the inner guidance; free of the so called humanly wishes of personal safety and joy.

In 2015, there was a great disaster of nature in Tamil Nadu. Do you know what happened then? A great calamity was experienced in Chennai and the cities around. Heavy flood situation was experienced; but even at that time, thousands of men and women came forward leaving their personal interests and safety behind. The most common people and the most eminent persons came together, without giving any importance to their own houses, their caste, creed, religion etc. and came forward to help each other. What was that thing inside them; which made them so strong and brave ?

Student: Oh Sir, it is unimaginable. It is beyond normal human attitude. But how Sir?

Teacher: Dears, it is this; that I want to explain. This is the real inner force- the strength of the inner self, the divine quality which sees no difference between human beings as for them; all are one -only humans like us; as on an individual level. And this is the divine quality; dormant in every human being. But, it is covered with the shadow of selfishness, greed, lust etc.

A selfless work stands above all and if all human beings understand that and live together for each other, then no calamity of any sort can destroy our oneness.

Those individuals; who are above these selfish demands are generators of that universal power, which is available for each human being on this earth & they always stand strong and satisfied.

Chapter 4: Points to remember

1. *Do not think of any inferiority in yourself or others.*

2. *Help others out if there are having any difficulty.*

3. *A selfless work stands above all.*

4. *A selfless worker stands strong and satisfied at all times.*

CHAPTER 5

Becoming free from anger and desire

The teacher had scheduled today's lesson in the backdrop of a beautiful sea shore. After enjoying and watching the waves hit the shore, the children turned to their teacher as he began his lesson: -

Teacher: Every one of us; dreams of becoming free and satisfied. For that; the first stage is to become aware of your lust and anger.

Student: Sir, many times desires and anger motivate us to do work.

Teacher: No, they are unsteady. You should not allow them to become your source of motivation.

Instead, try to perform action without any specific expectation.

Student: How can this be possible, Sir?

Action is not possible without expectation of result. Rather; action takes place to satisfy our expectation. I am confused about this.

Teacher: Dear, that's why; I brought you all near this sea shore today. Just observe the vastness of the sea. Do you hear the sound of the waves? And yet there is some quietude, isn't it? It is only in the calm that the 'inner self' works. The outer movement on the shore of the waves coming forward and again going back makes the sound. But the sea is silent and deep.

Like that; our senses bring up and down movements of lust and anger. These two are the main reasons for all inner fluctuations. If you are able to tame them, your actions can be pure, bringing no untoward effect; because the work is done without your personal expectations. Let personal gains be on the shore only. Remain unaffected by the tides like the vast sea.

Student: But, how do anger and lust hinder right action, Sir?

Teacher: See, I will tell you what happens when you work with anger and lust; which are only uncontrolled desires. When you get scolding for not getting good marks in exam, or you are not working well in some field of action, you get angry and say that; now I will show my mother or friend and that I can do this task well with this attitude- " I will show them for not having faith in me." But this 'showing

Chapter 5: *Don't get carried away with the waves of anger and desire; remain calm and then act.*

them' makes all the difference and you do the task; only to show off the task. When you do something just to show others, the results of such action are far more disastrous than even the actions that are done by normal desires. Perform well without any expectations of personal gain and it will be a right action

Student 1: It's fine to think like that Sir, but practically, it is not possible. How can one understand this?

Student 2: What is desire? How to identify it?

Teacher: Yes, yes. I will explain…

Student 3: But Sir, we have some basic needs, no?

Teacher: Yes, Yes! I will try to explain the questions. May I try and club up your questions?

Students: (*in chorus*) Yes sir.

Teacher: Ok. See, we all have some basic needs. Like; say clothes, even school dress, how many do we need? Two or three, maybe. But; we go on buying clothes more than what we need.

Say when we need a bicycle, do we have to go and get a racing bike?

Or even both? So, you see these sorts of desires are unknowingly fulfilled just for extra personal comfort. Some rich children may ask for a car and a driver, but we do not understand that; when the need goes beyond requirement, it gets into the category of comfort. Few; who have the ability to spend, go on buying cars for different occasions and this need then become luxury.

So; understand well your need and do not opt for comforts of any type. This comfort is a desire and if we go after a desire and if we don't get it we become angry and even fight with others, at times even our own parents. That disturbs the whole budget of the family and this desire enters in other children of the home and all get agitated. This is how anger and desire always spread around.

Student 1: Yes, sir. Now we understand the three, need, comfort and luxury clearly. As a student; we need to first look at our needs only and nothing more than basic needs.

Teacher: Yes. That is the attitude of good students. As you know that many students are deprived of even basic needs. When you observe and live like that, you can be peaceful and grow fast in making your personality stronger and stronger and also become more knowledgeable.

Chapter 5: Points to remember

1. *Perform your action without any expectation of returns.*

2. *Don't do anything to show off or to prove a point to anyone, but to grow.*

3. *Understand the difference between need, comfort and luxury.*

CHAPTER 6

Freedom and self-discipline

The venue for today's class was the National University campus which was known to be one of the best institutes of learning in the city. The enthusiasm of the students gathered in the lawn of the university was very contagious and after the students settled, the teacher began his lesson:-

Teacher: Children, I have brought you here today for a specific reason. This university is a place where knowledge is gained. The University teaches everybody, catering to each individual; irrespective of the person's status, caste, creed or religion. Today; the world has become so small and divided on many lines. One has to go beyond these petty thoughts and beliefs and think beyond compartments and think of the world at large.

These universities are recognized by other countries. Students come to universities from around the world and also many students go abroad, in other such universities to learn. One has to develop oneself into a universal personality and become global. Rising beyond personal identification, one must become a global student and a global personality. But to achieve all this, it is required to lead a disciplined life. How many of you like the word discipline?

Student 1: Sir, I do not like it as everyone at home or school asks us follow some discipline all the time.

Student 2: I; too; feel the same. I want to live as I feel. I want freedom and enjoy the freedom.

Teacher: I am talking about self–discipline first. You have to study, play, eat and do exercise as your duty towards yourself, isn't it? Or are you going to perform all this only after being told to do this by your parents or teachers?

No. You do it on your own; because it is clear that if you do not maintain discipline, in all these four, you will go astray. If somebody focusses on only one activity; like eating, sleeping, studying or exercising the whole day; then one may loose the chance of maintaining a balance of all these needs and will simply go astray.

Discipline is not always imposed upon us by others. We only have to develop it ourselves. This is the proper way to grow our personality.

Chapter 6: *If you are self-disciplined, nobody will have to impose discipline upon you.*

As far as your question of freedom, you want freedom; isn't it? Can I ask you, what do you want freedom from? First; you need to get freedom from the ignorance of not knowing and instead of being like birds; that are aimlessly flapping like chicken; having Vitamin B1 deficiency, try to understand the real meaning of freedom.

Freedom from the weakness of ignorance, includes knowing about keeping our body healthy and our mind sound; by understanding about the facts within and around us.

You may like the freedom; you seek for enjoyment; but ultimately, it will not create anything new. But, instead; your real productivity will be reduced to zero.

Student: Do we have to follow this at all times or can we follow it; only when we feel like?

Teacher: The answer is the same. If we live satisfied with our weaknesses and ignorance, we end up suffering. Is it not an advantage to know your shortcomings; when they are told to you? Isn't getting free from your weaknes the real freedom? Wouldn't you want to be free always?

Student: Yes sir, Now, it's clear. But, what; if discipline is imposed upon us?

Teacher: True! Some sort of discipline is imposed upon us. But one should take it by choice, for his or her growth and not as an imposition.

Ask any champion of wrestling, athletics, singing, dance, drama, military commandos or research scholars and they will tell you their personal stories of how, when they were under training of their masters, discipline was imposed upon them. Sportspersons bear unimaginable physical pressure, singers spend hours practicing day and night. Same is the case with those in the fields of dance and drama too.

They all accepted the discipline happily; for it was necessary for their growth. If they would have asked for freedom as per their will and whims, they would not have achieved this much of progress in their lives.

Student: Sir, explain in short for me. This discipline sounds horrible to me!

Teachers: See, maintain self-discipline first. Remain fit and accept the extra discipline by teachers and masters happily and not as an imposition; but as a requirement.

Student: Now, I understand it. But, is it necessary to do certain tasks every day at the same time with regularity?

Teacher: See, regularity always pays. It helps our body and mind to get channelized and give us the best output. You must have heard the phrase "a strong mind in a strong body". By this discipline; our tolerance increases and our physical, mental and emotional capacities also increase.

If all the sportsmen, artists, doctors, executives, teachers, military commanders do not follow any discipline, will you accept them? Same way; nobody will entertain an undisciplined person.

Lastly; observe the nature around you. The sun rises in the morning and moon in the evening, the wind flows all day and just as we work according to the discipline, nature too follows discipline.

At least; first become an ordinary human being to grow into an extra ordinary universal personality.

Chapter 6: Points to remember

1. *Discipline is not imposed, if you develop a self-discipline for your own development.*

2. *Prepare for real freedom from weakness and ignorance.*

3. *Learn discipline by observing Nature.*

CHAPTER 7

Nature's beautiful qualities

Today's session was organized in a beautiful and spacious garden. All the students were very happy to be in nature's company and a few guessed out aloud to the teacher that the topic of the session was connected to nature. The teacher nodded and then started the lesson:-

Teacher: Hi, students! How are you feeling in this new place? We are in this beautiful garden today to observe the unlimited creation of the great master of the universe. Human beings have a limited scope of creating such an environment. Tell me, what all do you see?

Student: The blue sky, trees and plants.

Teacher: Can you see some birds, butterflies and small insects?

Students: (Chorus) Yes, sir. All of them.

Teacher: You see nests, ant-hills etc. See that beautiful nest. Can you see the two baby birds, with flapping wings and open mouth eagerly waiting for the mother bird to feed them?

Student: Yes, Sir. It is so beautiful watching the mother bird feeding them.

Teacher: Can you guess who taught these birds to make a nest? To fly? To take proper food and save themselves from rain and heat?

So many creatures live here. Who do you think taught them to give birth to new generations and feed them? If you see, they have a language & signs of their own. Is there any class room like ours; where they learn it?

Student: No, Sir.

Teacher: See the beauty and unexpressed knowledge of nature and its creator. Do you know; the energy inside us is the same energy; which nurtures and allows nature to flourish in such an astonishing way?

Student: Yes, Sir. But human life is different from birds, animals and plants, isn't it?

Teacher: Right question my child! The secret is that; the same secret and unexpressed energy is in human beings also. The only difference is that; humans have a more

Chapter 7: *You have unlimited energy within you.*

developed mind. And that's why; it is our responsibility to help sustain this nature of which; we are also a part. Not disturbing this flora and fauna is the least we can do.

This very energy is present in water, fire, ether, wind, earth and all is made of the basic five elements. Even the sun, the moon, the stars "All is but His!". Whose? I am referring to the master of the universe and all is his creation.

Teacher: Look at the flowers. What do you see?

Student: There are white jasmines and red roses.

Teacher: Is it all? Go closer. Smell them.

Student: Oh, what a pleasant smell. Sir, it is really amazing. I love the smell of both.

Teacher: See the energising colours. They are different for each flower but; see the same earth is feeding them! What a secret marvel, isn't it? Don't you feel it?

Student: Yes, Sir. It is very energetic to be in this atmosphere. That's why our parents take us to parks and beaches. And now; you too; have brought us here.

Teacher: Yes, in the same way, the rising sun, glittering stars, rivers, mountains, sea shores and gardens; all give us energy. They are generators of nature giving you not only energy but also vastness to your thoughts. And that's why, we have to save them for our gains. We must never destroy them in any way. Instead, you must preserve and nurture them for yourself as their existence is for you only.

Remember; what is strong, beautiful and pleasant in nature is also present in strong men and women, commandos, writers, poets and individuals of great knowledge. All their qualities are because of this universal energy- and the same flows in all of us too. There is no difference. Only these heroes; whom we admire; have understood how to channelize it in a proper manner and grow into a universal personality.

Chapter 7: Points to remember

1. *You have unlimited energy within you but it remains unexpressed.*

2. *The energy of the five basic elements is present in you also.*

3. *Be always in the company of nature, physically as well as mentally.*

Chapter 8: *A balanced physical, mental and emotional being is essential.*

CHAPTER 8

The Key to success

The students were guided by the teacher into the city's best gymnasium; where various athletes were busy training in their specialised fields. The teacher instructed the students to observe the sports personnel from afar; without causing any disturbance in their training routine and then started the lesson: -

Teacher: Friends, as you have decided to be champions in your respective fields; I thought; I should bring you to this international gymnasium.

Student: Sir, why this gym? Any particular reason?

Teacher: See, this is the field; where champions exert a lot in improving their physical fitness. As such, basic requirements of concentration, consecration and devotion have to be fulfilled in any and all faculties. We have discussed earlier, But, I thought; you must see athletes performing in front of you.

Student: Yes, Sir! But what are these three requirements, you mentioned? Concentration, Consecration and Devotion?

Teacher: See; unless you concentrate on action, you can't even start progressing in any field. These athletes are performing physical acts that require good balance. A single mistake of not concentrating on their action will be disastrous for them. They might get hurt and have to take a long rest and waste the time of training and might ultimately loose the chance of getting perfection and will fall behind.

The second is consecration. If any athlete has any sort of fear while performing the task or during training, he cannot go ahead. So he must practice consecration- having a sort of complete faith in his trainer, his guidance and help. If he has that attitude, he can perform unexpectedly well in the task, and receive the master's help and guidance at all times. This is a basic requirement; while doing his tasks.

The third is devotion; which stands above these two qualities. You must have complete devotion and an unshakable faith in what you are doing. Devote time, energy and all interests for your goal.

If you follow these principles, you can be sure that you are meant to be a champion in your field.

Student: Sir, can you explain this more clearly for us?

Teacher: See, if you do not concentrate in studies; you will not remember anything while giving your examination. As a gymnast, if you don't concentrate, you will fall down. Even in all other activities of the day, if you do not concentrate, you may face an accident. So while talking, walking, eating, playing or any other activity; I can name many; concentration is a must. And, now you also; can understand that; this is the first requirement to achieve goals of any sort. Isn't it ?

Student: Yes, sir! It is clear. But, what about consecration and devotion?

Teacher: Oh! The second requirement; consecration; comes to help concentration. Consecration is offering yourself completely for the task you are performing. Unless; you offer yourself completely to the master, he cannot help you. If you are concentrating as per as your wish, but not offering your complete self to the master, how will he correctly guide you and bring out the hidden ability in you? That is why; consecration is important as the trainer knows best how to guide you. The last and most important is devotion. See, even if the master is there, the rest of the time you have to think on the task that you should do with devotion. First, devote time, then devote all your resources, and proceed completely ahead in devotion. And this; you have to inculcate by yourself only.

"A Knowledgable act done with devotion is the key".

Nothing remarkable can be achieved without concentration, consecration and devotion.

I, again; repeat "Knowledgeable act done with devotion is the only key for success."

Chapter 8: Points to remember

1. *A balance in physical, mental and emotional parts is essential for complete growth.*

2. *Try to remain aware of your physical, mental and emotional being.*

3. *A knowledgeable action done with devotion is the key for success in any field.*

CHAPTER 9

A prayer for transformation

Today's lesson was at an unusual venue. The students had assembled at a barren land. All the students wondered what could be learnt from such a place; that was bereft of any sort of flora or fauna. They all turned to the teacher; who then began the lesson in the unconventional location -

Teacher: Dear students, we have come here today; to this barren land. It is said and observed that very sparse or no plantation is possible on this land.

Student: Yes, Sir. This land is barren; since long. Even my grandfather; also; had told me that no one comes here. But; occasionally; we come to spend our time and enjoy the free air, play and go.

Teacher: Yes. But, can you imagine that if we take some efforts and give due consideration, concentrate and devote some time with faith, we can grow some plants that give fruits and vegetables?

Student: No, Sir. A few people tried; but miserably failed.

Teacher: Yes; that's what; I wanted to tell you, my friends. What was lacking in those efforts is first and foremost faith, work done without proper knowledge, concentration and devotion.

Student: How, Sir? Kindly explain us.

Teacher: A few tried; but not with a proper prayer.

Student: Means what? Prayers are there in religious places only!

Teacher: No. Not that sort of prayer. We learnt that, our land gives us food, trees, plants etc. in one sense. It is our source of life & hence we should also try to maintain and give life to this land as it is our mother. We call it our Nature-mother.

Student: So, are you saying that; just by praying, it will start giving us fruits and food?

Teacher: No! By prayer; I mean; by knowing and serving with devotion; we may grow many things. It will become fertile and give us food and fruits. We pray sincerely and she bestows her blessings in the form of food and fruits.

Chapter 9: *With efforts and devotion, cultivation can be done even on barren land.*

Student: But; how to grow on such a barren land?

Teacher: By adding manure. The soil will promote the growth of microbes, insects and worms. Their consistent movement will loosen the soil particles; thus making it more fertile. One may have to wait for a year or 2 and then one can plant vegetables; requiring minimum water and minimal enriched soil content. Then slowly; in some years; you can grow them aplenty. I have done it on my barren land; which got transformed and gave plenty of fruits and vegetables such as bananas pumpkins, flowers, papaya and more.

Student: Yes, but where is the prayer here?

Teacher: Dear, this is the real prayer! We are praying to the land to become fertile. We are taking efforts to make it fertile. Prayer is a give and take process; where you give your love, devotion and efforts. And the land gives you back; with love and blessings; in the form of food and fruit.

All this; you have to do with specific intention. Just work on making the soil fertile and you receive in the form of vegetation and not only you; but also the birds and other insects that in turn will make it more and more fertile.

And, this is the answer to your question on prayer. The prayer should be sincere with devotion; in what way you do and what you act. The means may be different but you will get the same benefit.

Doing all sorts of acts; sincerely; could be physical, mental and emotional prayers to the mother nature.

As a student your personality is also in a way barren! Initially, you are ignorant, weak and helpless to be of any help to your parents, society, nation and the world at large. But if you nurture yourself to be strong physically, mentally and emotionally; your parents, society and nation will get many things from you. Your constant prayers and efforts in this direction will make you an able person in many fields. And when you do this, do it with all the available resources you have. Do not wait for any specific shortage of any sort to be fulfilled. Whatever little means you have, accept it as a challenge and go ahead.

Chapter 9: Points to remember

1. *Caring for nature is also a way of prayer.*

2. *When you take care of the land with love and devotion, it blesses you in return by giving you fruits and food.*

3. *If resources are less, try to do your best with what you have. Even with less resources, you can achieve the same goal.*

CHAPTER 10

Nature's universal power and energy

After getting the requisite permissions from the school management and the parents, an excursion to a nearby hill-station was organized. The teacher then took the children to the famous botanical garden in the hill station and then began his session:-

Teacher: Dear friends, we experienced the light and power of the truth of nature when we visited the garden. Today we have come to this hill-station to understand the bigger part of the power of nature. What do you all observe from this great height?

Student: Sir, it is an amazing view - the big waterfall, the huge forest, the cool and fresh air. Even on the way, we saw many unknown plants and trees including herbal plants, plantations of different spices, different types of birds, honeycombs, butterflies. I can't explain the beauty of what I saw. I am going to write my experience in our journey to this hill station.

Teacher: Very good. You should all record this wonderful panorama.

Here is also a big botanical garden; which is for tourists and also for research students of agriculture and horticulture.

What is the energy behind this creation, it's beauty, strength and abundance of natural resources that benefit birds, animals and humans alike?

Student: Sir, this is the strength and wealth of the nature's creations for nature herself and also; for all living creatures around.

Teacher: Yes, my child. These are the three main parts of nature's creations- these three kingdoms; plant, animal and human kingdom. All are flourishing and helping each other.

Student: Yes, Sir. I can understand about plant and animal, but what about human kingdom?

Teacher: Why are you separating humans from these two? Probably, because you think human kingdom is different from the other two and that humans have an extra special source of energy and strength

Chapter 10: *Channelize the power inside you to receive more.*

Student: Yes, Sir.

Teacher: See, we all see the same strength in people around us. We think; it is different as we have a more developed mind than animal and the plant kingdom, isn't it?

Student: It is not clear, Sir. Please explain.

Teacher: See, certain people have extraordinary physical, mental and emotional skills. If you look at the scientists, who; with their research and efforts; gave us the knowledge of using energy for our betterment through various devices like electric bulbs, trains, aeroplanes and taught us to use our abilities and evolve from animal natured man to today's modern man. In all the great scientists across the world, we see common qualities; like selflessness and determination. Do you think, they have a common source; from where all the good qualities originated?

Student: I don't know, Sir.

Teacher: I told you this before. It is the same energy, flowing in plants, animals and human beings.

Student: If; it is the same, then why is there a difference between ordinary men and great men?

Teacher: It is the same secret. Great people channelize this power in them and so receive more. Like; everybody gets the same education in school and college, but few shine like stars and few hardly get through exams. Some have slow progress and those with more ability have more progress. They utilize it properly, that is the secret. Otherwise energy is the same for all and many get inspired from the lives of great personalities. One should have the inspiration and inclination to progress.

Student: Like Dr. A.P.J. Abdul Kalam, the hon'ble former President of India?

Teacher: Yes and not only scientists; army commandos, generals and knowledgeable persons in various fields and disciplines also. They are the path finders!

Student: Do all have the same energy?

Teacher: Yes, I told you the same. All energy is one. The single; all existing omnipresent energy is everywhere in all living and non-living things.

Student: How do you say non- living also, Sir?

Teacher: On rubbing the stones we see sparks and energy. This is then utilized in burning wood. The fire comes out; which is already present there inside wood in a dormant form. Seen or not seen, energy is always present inside all. So, take care of your plants and pets and at the same time also take care of the smallest things; like your pen and pencil, eraser and all the items which help you and give you comfort. Energy and life is everywhere, seen or unseen, felt or not felt.

Observe everything around you carefully and remain aware, careful and confident that you are in the company of energy everywhere.

Student: Yes, sir. Today, I think, all of us are feeling more energetic and confident. Thank you, sir.

Chapter 10: Points to remember

1. *Nature's strength is inexhaustible. The same is also found in humans and animals as well.*

2. *Channelize the power inside you to receive more.*

3. *Always be aware that there is oneness in all. Same energy is found in plants, animals, humans and non-living things as well.*

CHAPTER 11

The master stroke of a champion

Today's lesson was at the time of sunrise. All the childeren had assembled near a long green land with few trees to watch the bright rising sun. After reminiscing their joyous visit to the botanical garden atop the hill station, one of the students asked a burning question, that had arisen while discussing with her fellow classmates: -

Student: Sir, all that you taught us till now is great, but how do we implement this knowledge in practical life. It seems difficult to follow and practice all the time.

Teacher: Yes. I wanted only this from you; because understanding the ideals may be joyous but to achieve it could seem to be a dream today. If we follow some psychological and emotional aspects and tame our mind; it could become easy.

Student: Means what, Sir? I understood nothing, Sir.

Teacher: Ok, Ok. No issues. See, to achieve our ideal; we have to observe and identify the hurdles on the way of progress. The first requirement to become an ideal student is that he or she must be free from desire and hatred and then perform actions.

Student: Yes, but can you highlight the same with examples; so that we can; not only understand; but also perform?

Teacher: Oh, great! The "Will to do" is the foremost requirement and you have shown a willingness to perform. See, if you are playing in a particular tournament, play as per the rules of the game, concentrate on your performance and team work, putting aside any personal dispute that you may have had with any of the team members. Do not play with hatred or strong feelings of desire of showing off your own game to your team members or to the other team's members. Simply, be away from desire or hatred in any act you do, just play for the joy of playing and giving your best for the entire team.

Do not do any act in life to show off or to prove it to somebody. Instead, try to bring perfection in action.

Student: Yes, Sir. Now it is clear.

Chapter 11: *Be sincere, remain quiet, do your work as best as you can.*
This is all that is wanted from a champion.

Teacher: Students; we have learnt about the sun, its great light that gives life to plants, animals and humans. But, do you know; there are many such suns?

Student: No, Sir! Our galaxy has one sun, many moons and stars.

Teacher: See, scientists and astronomers have proven that there are many galaxies and many suns.

Student: So many suns; sounds horrible, Sir. We can't see even the one bright sun that we know with our naked eyes. If, we do that we get dark spots in our eyes.

Teacher: Imagine; if we see many of them at a time?

Student: Not possible to even think of it, Sir. Our body will not exist, if we face many suns.

Teacher: Same way, if we think of the many vast galaxies with the many suns that you call horrible, we become silent in respect of their vastness and feel very tiny in front of the universe.

Student: Sir, we can't tolerate one sun. How can we even think of seeing all of them?

Teacher: Yes, but you have to understand the essence of the sun. The energy of the sun that you see. When you understand that the light of the sun and light in you in the form of energy is the same, then what do you think?

Student: It gives a great, great feeling and I feel powerful. But, if we are the same energy, how can we sustain?

Teacher: My dear, the energy in sun is huge. But, the same energy inside of us is as a spark only. And it gets shadowed; when we are overcome by our desires and hate for something or someone.

Student: But sir, we must hate what is bad and ugly, isn't it?

Teacher: See, there is a difference between hate and dislike. A feeling of liking for good and great things is always present. But, there should be no hate inside, even for what is bad and ugly.

Student: How, Sir?

Teacher: See, one may have likes and dislikes. It is your personal freedom and choice to have preferences; which are most natural. But, when you develop a hate for a particular person or a thing, then the emotions produce a negative reaction inside you and then this becomes a great hurdle. Keep aside your hate or repulsive feeling for something you do not like. One can have likes and dislikes as per one's choices. One may not like a particular dish, e.g. Brinjal and it is perfectly okay to dislike something, but one should never have hate for anything or any person for any matter.

Hate; only harms the inner harmony and creates imbalance inside and is the biggest hurdle in the path of progress. Remember to remain calm and do your work as best as you can. This is all that is expected from a student.

Student 1: Oh, now it is clear and I now understand the difference between disliking and hating a person or a thing.

Student 2: Yes, sir. It is our duty to understand that spark within us and remove the clouds of ignorance. We must let it work freely for our development and help us grow from an individualistic selfish personality into a universal personality.

Teacher: Very good children. This is going to create a strong base for your overall personality development. Manifest the same light by performing right action and bringing out the champion inside of you.

To sum it up, perform all actions; devoid of any specific desire or expectations. This is the true and perfect way of performing actions; A desire less action; is the master stroke of a champion; who works untouched by any impulsive reactions whatsoever.

Chapter 11: Points to remember

1. *If you can perform any act without hate and desire, you can do unimaginably well in any field.*

2. *Do not do anything; just to show others. Do it as you like to do it for yourself.*

3. *Be sincere, remain quiet, do your work as best as you can. This is all that is wanted from a champion.*

CHAPTER 12

Recognizing the master of the universe

For today's lesson, the parents of the students were asked to drop their wards in the evening time for a sixty-minute session; where they would be observing the moon and the various constellations visible in the sky. The students were very happy to meet their friends for this fun activity and began talking among themselves about the unique experience they had in this workshop. They unanimously concluded that their teacher was a master and they decided to formally announce their conclusion to their teacher:-

Student 1: Sir, we all have started thinking about you as a master and true teacher!

Student 2: Yes, sir. We know that people in all fields like sports, drama, singing and all other sciences; such as chemistry, physics, astronomy and many disciplines have been trained by masters of their fields.

Student 3: Sir, before today's class, we all were discussing about you. The way you have been guiding us is unique and all encompassing. Your teaching is universal and without focussing on any specific field, you are teaching us; how we can become champion students of any and all faculties.

Sir, can we say that you are our teacher and master and we are your disciples?

Teacher: See, friends! It is your choice to consider me as a teacher or see me as a master. But, I consider myself as your friend by choice. I want to keep up this relationship of a friend because there is a freedom in friendship. And, this relation makes both of us free from any undue pressures and creates a good atmosphere for learning and teaching.

Student: Yes. That's why, we feel free to ask questions and learn from your friendly answers.

Teacher: Yes, this is how we can remain united and at the same time; enjoy our personal freedom as well.

Student: Yes, we are now ready to learn further about this universal subject.

Teacher: Students, now look up. What do you see? We observe; the sky is slowly getting darker and the milky white stars are glittering brighter. The atmosphere seems quiet and as we go on observing, this vastness of the sky and glittering stars, we; too; become silent, isn't it? It is only in the calmness, that the higher mind can

Chapter 12 *Every champion practices silencing of the mind by offering it to the master of the universe.*

work. So, let us meditate on the highest light inside and outside us and pray for greater strength and knowledge. Let us pray that we; be bestowed with greater power and wisdom.

Student: Yes, Sir. This is called connecting to a formless source of energy.

Student: But, many worship and pray to some or the other forms.

Teacher: Very good. You are both right. It depends solely upon an individual's perception of the source-the formless or a form.

Student: But, which is right, Sir?

Teacher: Both are right; as per the individual's choice.

Student: Sir, then which is the better choice?

Teacher: See, the truth is- the formless only takes form. So, both ways are good for the person. It is as per his or her choice.

Student: But, results of one's choice shall also differ, isn't it?

Teacher: See, my friend, what is important; is the faith, with which you pray and not the object of prayer- formed or formless.

That's why, we are here. In this quiet place, you can introspect; where your devotion lies-for the master of the universe or the teachings found in it.

It doesn't matter; whether your devotion is for a form or formless. The main aspect is your trust; with which you are following a truth. The whole nature is there before you and the deep faith inside you is there to guide you.

Student: Sir, this is not very clear. Can you share some example?

Teacher: See, every child has a firm faith in his or her mother. The child may ask something with a deep urge and the mother fulfils.

But, sometimes a child pretends and throws tantrums, but the mother is very clever and understands that the child doesn't need it. All the prayers or urges expressed by the child through pleading requests, crying or even shouting goes in vain and seems futile.

Why do you think? The simple reason is that, the reason for which the child is praying is not so important as the sincerity of the urge.

Student: Yes, I understood the means and ways followed in praying are not of that much importance; but the original urge and sincerity is what matters. True sincerity pays.

Teacher: Please, do not pretend to do, but Be! The ways can be many. You can sit or stand in a particular way while praying; as they are various physical postures. But, do not pose, be sincere.

Student: Yes, this is understandable. But are there particular timings for prayers, or particular places for worship?

Teacher: There are no specific timings or places. Prayers can be done at any time and at all times and all places.

Student: For prayers, one must be silent. Sir, I think this is the most difficult thing for me, so, it means; it is not possible at all.

Teacher: Yes, but by practice, you can achieve this normal condition. Today, you find it difficult because your mind is never silent and is only wavering.

Student: Sir, how? What are the ways to do so?

Teacher: See, first of all, you must try to sit quietly; at least in a relaxed physical posture. Let the mind be free as you achieve this quiet physical posture. This quiet sitting will only bring silence in your physical. Many say they can't sit quietly for a minute also.

Student: Ok, Sir, what about the mind?

Teacher: Just remember these stars or the quiet sea or even the trees and concentrate your thoughts upon them and slowly the mind shall also be quiet, at least for that time. I have told you before, you must develop a sound mind in a sound body. When you are quiet, your body and mind, both shall become quiet after sometime.

Student: Oh, I find it very difficult to be quiet, Sir. Especially; when I have so many things to do.

Teacher: Then, at least whatever you do, do without expectations. When you are studying, helping others, playing or whatever action that you are doing, do them with no specific desire and see how thoughts are minimised as you focus on the works.

Student: Ok Sir, I do understand now. Whenever we do something, we must not expect any reward for it and have no desire before, during and afterwards. This way, we simply become detached from these desires and expectations. This itself brings in a natural quietude and satisfaction.

Teacher: Yes, my boy. Actually life is simple. We make it difficult with unwanted desires, hates and cravings.

Every champion practices silencing of mind; either by exercise for body and mind or by offering it to the master of the universe or remembering the source and offering at every moment; at least by self-discipline; along with a 'right mental attitude' (R.M.A) as explained earlier. But, if they follow this, then they can live happily in all good and so called bad times. By leading with example and passing on this knowledge; from generation to generation, it will bring delight in their lives. This delight is beyond pleasure and pain.

Chapter 12: Points to remember -

1. *Be sincere, not serious. It is sincerity; that pays. So, don't ever pretend to be sincere, always be sincere.*

2. *Detached actions bring quietude in oneself.*

3. *Life is simple. Desires, hate and lust make it complicated.*

Chapter 13: *Be aware of your surroundings.*

CHAPTER 13

Know Thyself- Becoming aware of oneself.

For today's lesson, the students had assembled in their class room again. Some of the students had pulled up long faces as they were expecting a lesson outdoor. Catching the mood of the students, the teacher began the lesson: -

Teacher: Dear friends; today, we have gathered here, in our usual place; that we know very well, our class room! Do you know why? Because, we have to concentrate upon our individual self and personality.

Student: Oh, I thought we were going to visit outside. Why not outside sir ?

Teacher: See, we are going to visit a big and beautiful place, which is not outside, but is inside us. Do you know our individual self is not less than any deep sea, huge mountain range, dense forest or the vast sky?

Student: That is interesting, Sir. It is not something; I ever thought of.

Teacher: You must have heard these wise words "Know thyself" as one of the principles for self-training. This is very important because we are always looking outwards and outside but we do not give more importance to ourselves on the inside. If the outside is a vast field to learn from, the same way it is necessary to understand, everything about our own personality on the inside too.

Student: Sir, How is the great field that is outside equal to our tiny personality?

Teacher: See, we are a part of this great universe, though a part, we are also complete; like the whole of nature that is outside us.

Student: Kindly explain clearly, Sir.

Teacher: First of all, you have to be aware about yourself. Suppose, you are roaming on a cricket ground and suddenly, a ball comes on to you when you are unaware?

What happens? you get hurt isn't it? But, if at such a moment, you are aware and alert, you get out of the range, dodge the ball and save yourself from getting hurt.

Student: Yes, sir.

Teacher: And, further understand this. Our small being is also a complete universe in itself- a part of the universe and to become a champion; we must know ourselves better first.

Student: Sir, some details about this please.

Teacher: See, our body is made up of 5 elements, 5 senses of action and 5 senses of wisdom, mind, intellect and ego. And beyond all is the "energy".

Student: How can we understand, Sir?

Teacher: When we travel outside, our eyes tell us about a bad road and then, we change our route and use a smoother road. Now; though we have eyes, if; without noticing, we take the bad road only, then we will get hurt. The same way, if we are alert we can sense from the atmosphere that it is going to rain and then take proper care to carry an umbrella with us.

Student: Ok, Sir.

Teacher: When we eat, we must be aware of what we eat. We must ensure that it is nutritious also and not just satisfying our sense of taste.

Student: Sir, we understand that awareness is important, but how can we understand about the elements and senses of action in detail?

Teacher: See; we as an individual can consider ourselves to be as a vast field. The five elements are earth, fire, wind, water and sky.

They are present all across the universe and we also communicate with the universe through our senses of wisdom - eyes, ears, nose, tongue and skin and the sense organs which enable us to perform the acts like seeing, listening, smelling, tasting and touching. Also there is another thing inside of us that we call the mind. Hence understanding our body and mind is of foremost importance.

Student: Yes, Sir. By becoming aware of the five elements, five senses of working and action and five sense of wisdom. And; above that, the mind.

Teacher: Yes! And now you understand that we; as humans; are; also; a part of this universe. We are a part of this creation, the creator; though aloof; is present in this creation as nature is nothing but the consciousness; which can be called the executive power of the universe.

Student: Oh, its clear; but even then; we see separateness in one and every individual.

Teacher: That's the main thing, inside every individual irrespective of any such discrimination, there is the same presence of the creator. An immortal energy resides in this mortal body. Whoever understands this, is the wise knower and such a person feels the equality in all living things and understands this ultimate truth.

Student: But, how Sir?

Teacher: He understands that just like the velocity of the wind, in the centre of a storm is zero, behind all chaos and activity, behind the play of forces of the universe; there is a silent supreme orderliness. And; hence; those; who understand this truth are not burnt by the flames of passion and for such a person, the greatest status is certainly assured.

Chapter 13: Points to remember

1. Remain conscious at all times.

2. Become aware of your senses.

3. Nature is nothing but the executive power of consciousness.

Chapter 14: *Peacefulness is progressive. Restlessness and laziness is regressive.*

CHAPTER 14

The Three traits in everyone

For today's session, the teacher took all the students to the assembly hall. A function had just got over for the students of another batch and so the students from other batches were scattered around. The teacher gathered his students to one side of the assembly hall and began his lesson:-

Teacher: Students, we are in the assembly hall today. The reason is that; I want to show you the difference between a classroom and an assembly gathering. In a compact place or classroom with limited number of students, we try to keep silence, and maintain an obedient posture and sit attentively, isn't it?

Student: Yes, Sir. We; all; do that and try to keep ourselves in discipline as we feel; we may be otherwise caught for being mischievous and punished.

Teacher: That's it. But, what happens in an assembly hall ?

Student: It is a big place and the number of students is much more; as all students from all classrooms assemble here.

Teacher: Yes and your class teacher can't notice each and every student and so; students feel a bit relaxed. But, do you know, each student behaves as per his/her temperament or inborn properties?

Student: What properties, Sir? Can you explain?

Teacher: Yes; but for that, first; we have to understand the properties that are naturally present in all.

Student: How and why, Sir ?

Teacher: Wait, wait! Do not become impatient. First, know the properties of nature and then their close relation with individuals. Nature causes three basic properties to be present in all.

Student: What are those properties, Sir?

Teacher: The three properties are the Restless, Lazy and Peaceful natures found in individuals. They are present in all of us. Just observe, what is going on in the assembly hall. Everybody is busy with his/her nature. Few are restless and just running, some are standing aloof; leaning onto a pillar and some are just quiet and observing around. They are working as per their natures.

Student: Sir, kindly explain in a simple way so that we can understand it.

Teacher: Ok. Tell; me what do you observe among the students there?

Student1:   Sir, that boy is continuously moving out of line.

Student 2:   Yes, sir. One is yawning.

Student 3:   Sir, some are standing quietly.

Teacher: What else can you observe?

Student: Sir, the two boys are fighting over there and two girls there are pulling and pushing each other.

Teacher: So, in many students, we see different traits and natures; isn't it?

Students: (in chorus): Yes, Sir!

Teacher: We see that some children are restless, some are silent and some are lazy. We observe these traits in ourselves too. But; it is fluctuating, isn't it? Sometimes you are restless, sometimes you are calm and peaceful & sometimes very lazy.

Students: (in chorus): Yes, Sir!

Teacher: Here, you see; we have to observe these traits and try to balance them.

Student: How, Sir?

Teacher: Observe, when do you get restless? Every time you do something you do not like or if someone you don't like comes in front of you, or when you react strongly or when you have strong likes and dislikes. We can't accept anything that goes against our will and so become restless. But, this restlessness further shakes hands with anger. Initial restlessness further increases and gets transformed into anger and then you also become angry. You must have noticed that restless children suddenly become angry, isn't it?

Student: Yes, Sir. When my mother gives me something which I don't like, I get angry.

Teacher: This is because of your restless nature. And; in class also, some students do not listen to the class because they are restlessly doing something else. And then, they get into trouble. Because of this restless nature and impatient behaviour, you have poor tolerance. You get into unwanted discussions and it results in fights and in such a disturbed mind, you experience unhappiness.

Student: Sir, but little restlessness is ok, no?

Teacher: See, sometimes restless children do big things also. But; not all the times. Restlessness to achieve things quickly as per particular expectations leads to negative results. This is because; doing things with expectation; brings sorrow when the expectations are not fulfilled.

Student: Ok, Sir, I understand it now.

Teacher: If you look at some children, they are always very peaceful. They quietly listen to the class, they attend workshops, do their work silently and peacefully. They like to seek knowledge. They want to learn more they are contented and even help others; instead of troubling them. They are the right representatives of the peaceful nature.

Student: Got it Sir, what about the lazy nature?

Teacher: Sometimes; we don't do any work or we simply don't feel like doing anything. We find no enthusiasm and feel like just lying down or simply sleeping. At times, we feel like we don't even want to think of starting anything and in this state of inertia, we do not accept our mistakes. These are the traits of those having a lazy nature.

Student: But; how do we come out of the lazy and restless natures and have a peaceful nature?

Teacher: See; first; you have to observe these traits in you. All three are present in us. Apply (RMA) 'Right Mental Attitude' and create a conducive atmosphere in your personality. Eat a proper diet, have proper rest and sleep. Then you will feel enthusiastic and full of energy in your daily life. Use all your enthusiasm in helping your parents, friends and other needy people and you will observe that your restlessness; too; can be used in a constructive activity. Laziness; when channelled correctly; can be used for getting good rest and regulated sleep. With your efforts; you will slowly improve and develop a peaceful nature which will bring a feeling of peace in school, college, at home and with all your friends. When you are peaceful inside, you will find that friends, family and teachers- all these three groups shall start taking interest in you and will be more and more helpful to you. In this state, all three natures inside you will be in creative restlessness, creative restfulness and progressive peacefulness.

Student: Yes, Sir. This sounds very good. We feel; this lesson is a dissection of our three natured personality & now we see it differently and we will use them for a collective good.

Chapter 14: Points to remember -

1. Become aware of your individual nature.

2. Three types of natures found in all are restless, lazy and peaceful natures.

3. Observe these traits and work closely on yourself.

CHAPTER 15

The purpose of hurdles and difficulties

For today's lesson, the teacher took his students out for a field trip to a paddy field. In the fresh atmosphere of the paddy field, the teacher began the lesson:-

Teacher: Students; we are near a paddy field, today.

Student: Yes, Sir! It is so nice to see the farm with fully grown paddy.

Teacher: Correct. What else do you see here? You are holding a fully grown paddy in your hand. What do you think is the next step?

Student: They are ready now and good to eat after a good cleaning.

Teacher: Yes, we eat the upper part. But, what about the middle and the roots below?

Student: It is just waste, Sir. We can't eat it.

Teacher: It seems to be waste for human consumption; but, you know the middle part; which is big; is used as fodder for animals like cows and buffaloes; as it is good for their sustenance and growth. The lowest part is returned to the soil; which becomes a source of nutrients for the soil itself.

Student: So nice! So; nothing goes waste. Upper part is utilized by humans, middle for cattle and last for soil- as a return gift.

Teacher: Indeed! Now; just come close and observe the paddy in the field. What do you see?

Student: The grains are fully grown, but I observe some small insects on it.

Teacher: Yes. These insects are seasonal. They appear at a particular time. You can also see the small birds eating these insects. These seasonal insects are; also; the food for birds. There is a food chain in process. What we all see here is not a random creation; but a purposeful food chain, isn't it?

Student: Yes, Sir.

Teacher: So; what seems to be just random insects or birds, on the surface level, is actually a closely knit ecosystem functioning here.

Chapter 15: *There is a definite plan behind all creation.*

Student: Yes, Sir; it seems like a plan of nature. Other than this food chain, can you share any other example, Sir?

Teacher: Yes, there is a same system in ocean also. So many fishes are there. The small ones eat algae & small insects; whereas the big ones eat the small ones and the big are eaten by the still bigger fishes. This is a self-sustaining food chain in the oceans.

Student: Oh, great! We do not feed the oceanic fishes as well.

Teacher: The same way, there is an ecosystem on the land as well. Among the animals, a few eat grass, leaves and plants; the bigger animals eat the meat of smaller animals and the big ones; too; are eaten by the mightier ones; like the tigers and panthers. This ecosystem self sustains and still new ones are born in time's course and grow. We do not feed them as well.

Student: Oh, what a scientific cycle of the nature!

Teacher: Beyond these examples, there are huge and unimaginable wonders which we can marvel at. Just observe the glittering stars, the moon and the sun. The sun is the strongest object giving light to all these objects in our galaxy. But, still we know that some stronger object is giving light to our galaxy; also; and many more galaxies; like ours; are present in the whole of the universe.

Student: Oh, it is really unimaginable!

Teacher: Yes, but; the truth is that; there is a true and a definite purpose behind the workings of the universe. When we observe these things, we come to know that there is a perfect plan of a highest creative power; which is visible behind all of these and; also; behind all the chaos in our life.

Student: Can you make it easy for us to understand?

Teacher: See, when you are small, others feed you and when you grow up, you have to manage on your own and feed others too.

A farmer grows food and offers to many. A young boy learns when he is a child; but grows up and becomes a teacher. We; all; must; in our respective fields, learn, experience and pass on the knowledge to the next generation and play our own roles in the same way; so that the chain moves on and on in all fields.

Student: Yes, Sir. But, we face many difficulties and hurdles! What is the sensible plan or purpose behind that?

Teacher: See, there is a definite plan for bringing an evolution in us. Through hurdles, physical and emotional strain, we become stronger. See; the great personalities never had an easy life. The hurdles are part of a plan that is in place for our training.

Student: But, it could be for the great ones, but, what for an ordinary person like me?

Teacher: Who says you are an ordinary person? See, you are like you. You are distinct. Nobody is exactly like you. There may be someone; similar in appearance, but your palm impressions are different and unmatchable.

Student: Yes, Sir. That's why, these impressions are meaningful in finding out a particular person.

Teacher: When you understand this difference in the physical aspects, just think of the different thoughts and functioning of the mind, which is far more difficult to comprehend than these physical impressions.

Student: Yes, Sir. It means that every individual is different and a master of his own self.

Teacher: Yes and so the hurdles and difficulties come with a purpose.

Student: What purpose?

Teacher: Purpose of making you stronger and stronger. That's why; we are learning these key points to be mastered; so that; we grow in a right and progressive way to achieve the highest.

In previous classes, you have learnt to become strong physically, mentally and emotionally, and these are the key words to be observed and followed in life. The ultimate aim of our life is to grow and progress.

Chapter 15: Points to remember

1. *Study the different types of food chains in the ecosystem.*

2. *There is a definite plan behind; even; the chaos in our life.*

3. *You are like yourself, unique and there is nobody in the world like you.*

4. *The ultimate aim of life is to grow and progress.*

CHAPTER 16

Encouraging the positive and eliminating the negative traits

For today's lesson, the teacher took the students out to a very unusual venue; which none could have ever guessed. For their educational excursion, the students had arrived at the Government prison building and after all the formalities were completed, the students assembled around their teacher and the lesson began:-

Teacher: Students, you have mentally understood the difference between good and bad. But; now; we are here to observe practically the consequences of bad action, right before your eyes.

Student: Sir, today, you have brought us to Government prison! I didn't expect you to bring us here. Why here, Sir?

Teacher: I have brought you here to show you the condition of the prisoners. Do you know why they are here?

Student 1: Those; who do wrong; are sent to prison.

Student 2: Sir, I have heard prisoners are bad people!

Teacher: But, how do they do wrong?

Student: They engage in some unsocial activity.

Teacher: Like?

Student: They steal, cheat and do physical harm to others.

Teacher: Why do they do so?

Student: Please explain it, sir. We only know that they are bad.

Teacher: But; when born; they were also like other children; innocent, like all kids are. Do you know, a prisoner can teach us; something; in a better way than a good teacher?

Student: How is that, Sir?

Chapter 16: *What is constructive and positive is good. All that is destructive and negative is bad.*

Teacher: Good people teach us to do good and behave in a good manner. But, we are at times reluctant or feel like, it takes a lot of trouble to become like that.

But; here; the prisoners show us directly; as if saying- "If you do as we did, your condition will also be like us". As they are here; their family, friends and society are all suffering. They were handcuffed in front of all; when they were taken to prison. Even though the meals are provided for their sustenance, the miserable faces filled with regret; directly tell us what not to do. Instantly, it pricks our conscience and mind like a sudden injection.

While, we often learn theory of doing good things and forget it, here is a practical lesson that seeing even once, you remember forever.

Student 1:   Yes, sir. We learnt many things in the different places we visited with you, but this is a direct practical lesson about the principle "why we should not follow the wrong path or do bad".

Student 2:   But, why does this happen, sir? If we know it in principle, can we not check or prevent it?

Teacher: See, there are so called good and bad traits and we all have some traits which aren't good in a small percentage. Sometimes, we behave as good children and sometimes as bad children.

Student: Is it so? Do we have both?

Teacher: Yes and mostly it depends upon the overall nature.

Student: How does one identify the overall nature, Sir?

Teacher: See, those who have a good nature do not hurt others. They are contented with what they have. They are happy and satisfied and do not want more and more. They are not greedy and have no such desires to accumulate things. They; also; do not always find faults in others. They are peaceful, they want to seek knowledge, to improve upon their physical, mental and emotional sides. They feel no jealousy for anybody; but concentrate on their own personality and try to better their personality by subtracting their weaknesses of all sorts and by improving upon their good traits.

Student: Oh, yes; they are good; but, who are considered bad?

Teacher: People; who are aggressive, arrogant and carrying false ego are considered to be of bad nature. They are greedy, always after money and full of unending desires. They believe in only seeking pleasure and for getting that they may cheat others, grab their properties. They have no other purpose of life other than this and they do not bother about consequences of their actions and do not even care; if they hurt others physically or emotionally.

Student: Oh, Sir! Does this mean, we have a hidden evil inside of us?

Teacher: No, we do not have a hidden evil inside. See, we have desires in us and when they are not fulfilled, we loose our peace of mind. Instead of remaining happy, we very strongly want to fulfil them by any way possible. When, we can't fulfil them, it gives birth to anger and we adopt even bad ways to fulfil desires. We beg, borrow, or steal or snatch things; that we want and at times even physically hurt others. Those; who walk this path; often end up in such prisons.

Student 1: Oh! Now we understand why you brought us here! Really, sir. We now practically understand, what not to do!

Student 2: Sir, but what should we do to control the bad traits in us.

Teacher: See; this very word 'control' is not required.

Student: Why, sir?

Teacher: See, when you impose a control from outside or inside of any sort, it gives birth to a repulsive and reactionary force that creates all sorts of problems.

Student: Then, what to do with such traits of desire, anger, jealousy ?

Teacher: First, observe them and then quietly try to minimise these traits.

Student: But; how, Sir? If I am hungry and want to eat, is it not a desire?

Teacher: This is what, we have to understand. We must learn to differentiate a genuine need from an unwanted desire. Anything, that is more than what you need is bad.

Observe this inside of you and don't go after fulfilling your every desire; because they go on increasing; but never get fulfilled. This; then; leads to anger and then hate and all these ultimately push you away from the right path, from good to bad.

Student: Sir, so will bad people remain bad always?

Teacher: No, that is not true. Bad can become good and vice versa. If one steals and feels bad about it and apologises and repents for the act by deciding not to repeat it again in life, he can be transformed into a good person. Likewise, if a good person, due to a rush of desires does something wrong; like stealing and allows that desire to continue inside, he goes astray.

So, remember children; do no try to impose a control by force. Instead, observe the traits within and remove the negative ones and concentrate upon improving the good traits. Good is constructive and positive. Bad is destructive and negative. Remember these words. They will help you throughout life. Best wishes, my friends.

Chapter 16: Points to remember

1. *The consequences of bad actions are directly shown to us by the inmates of a prison. In this aspect, prisoners are the best teachers; who teach us what we shouldn't do.*

2. *Instead of rigidly crushing or exercising forceful control on desires, observe them and minimize your traits.*

3. *What is constructive and positive is good. All that is destructive and negative is bad.*

Chapter 17: *Choose the right type of food.*

CHAPTER 17

Choosing the right food

For today's lesson the venue was no surprise, the teacher had already announced that he would be treating the students at the food court and that their lesson would start after they enjoyed eating their choice of food. On reaching the venue, the teacher said:-

Teacher: Hi students, you all must be very happy today.

Students (in chorus): Yes, sir. This is a surprise party for all of us.

Student 1: I see so many types of food dishes here that I can't decide what to eat sir.

Student 2: Oh, all of these are mouth-watering items.

Student 3: This is the most famous food court of our town.

Student 4: Sir, what is the purpose behind bringing all for us here?

Teacher: The first purpose is that I am happy; observing your progress; in the last few days. You are acquiring knowledge for personality development with sincerity by asking real questions, suitable for your growth. You are not just asking informational queries; but are asking to know something truly. That's why, I have arranged this party.

Student: We understand that and we are enjoying this party and your love for us; but you always teach us something; wherever we go.

Teacher: Yes, rightly understood. But tell me your choice from these dishes first.

Student 1: Sir, I would like to take anything sweet.

Student 2: Sir, I want to opt for the crispy fries.

Student 3: I will go with idli and sambar.

Teacher: Ok, Ok. Let's first start and finish eating. After everybody is satisfied, we shall sit nearby and discuss on some vital points. Ok ?

Students (in chorus): Okay sir, Thank you Sir.

After enjoying various dishes as per their own liking, all students gathered.

Student: Sir, now we are ready to know something from you.

Teacher: See, we all know about the restless, lazy and peaceful nature in individuals; isn't it? Likewise, even the food; that we eat; is having properties to enhance these qualities in us.

Student: Ok, so food is also of three types? Please, explain.

Teacher: You have observed many types of foods here. All the foods are categorised into mainly three types.

Student: How, sir?

Teacher: See; 1st type of food is fresh, easy to digest nourishing for our body and is neither oily nor spicy. Eating this type of food makes one happy and peaceful.

The 2nd type of food is extra spicy, salty, oily and difficult for digestion. Consuming such foods cause diseases in the long run and by eating such foods one becomes restless.

The 3rd category of food is the lowermost type of food. It comprises of stale, uncooked or half cooked food or foods having a foul smell. This is bad for heath and produces a feeling of laziness in the eater.

Student: So, we must know; what we eat and we must eat it very carefully, isn't it, sir?

Teacher: Very good. Yes, we must observe what we eat. If; at times; you eat heavily on some occasion, then you must either observe a fast or take very light food and balance the diet subsequently. This way you can keep yourself healthy and happy.

Student: This, we will definitely follow, sir.

Teacher: And further; what you eat produces the effect in your nature also. If you eat simple and fresh food, you feel calm. If you eat spicy and hot food, you feel restless and if you eat the stale old food, you become lazy.

Student: Sir, what about non vegetarian food?

Teacher: See; veg or non-veg, the basic principle is the same. Food is food and whatever food at home is made for you is always good, as it always made with love and for your own good. But students, we are studying the basic principles and types of foods. So, one should never pronounce on another's food. As we have learnt before, there are likes and dislikes in all human beings. They are always there. An individual's freedom to choose one's own food as per his or her likings should be considered.

At the same time, one must make the best choice of food for achievement of progress in both-health and nature.

All the best students. Good day!

Chapter 17: Points to remember

1. *Food and nature have a close relation.*

2. *Food is food. Other's food choices shouldn't be our primary concern.*

3. *Healthy food is that; which is digestible easily. Food should be well cooked, neither burnt nor raw.*

Chapter 18: *You have to respect the four pillars of the society and also respect each other.*

CHAPTER 18

The Four pillars of the society

Today's lesson was scheduled at school and four very important guests representing the four pillars of the society were invited to share their experience with the students. The teacher announced to the children:-

Teacher: Dear Students, I am happy that all the students of class are present today.

Students (in chorus):   We all are eager to know more, Sir.

Teacher: Dear ones; today, I have invited a few guests; who are very experienced and shall share their experience with all of us.

Student: Oh! That's great. We are eager to see and hear them.

Teacher: Listen students, I once again request you all to be calm and grasp the most vital points from our four guests; who are from four different backgrounds but are together helping in the construction of a strong society and strengthening the four basic pillars of an evolved society.

Every child is born with a definite liking and choice as per his or her inherent nature. So, the child should not be labelled as per his family, community or any other reason whatsoever. Taking birth in a specific family line is not as much important as the duties done by the individual. Any individual; who works selflessly and with dedication is respected by the society; which has four pillars.

Student: Means? Sir, what four?

Teacher: For many generations, the society is run by four categories:-

1. Providers

2. Carers

3. Teachers

4. Protectors

Student: Yes, sir. Is this like the rigid system that divides people on caste?

Teacher: No, No. As members of an evolving society, we should change this mentality and not discriminate on the basis of caste or any other rigid labels.

Student: But, how sir?

Teacher: The change should always start with yourself first.

Student: What will happen; if I; alone; start thinking and behaving. Others will oppose me and I shall be left out of society alone.

Teacher: This is only your fear; but you don't have to think this way at all. Have no fear; when you cling to the truth. Also the society too is changing.

Student: But, this may take a very long time and we shall suffer by the opposition in the society.

Teacher: Across the world, every change is always met with opposition. Even; in the most developed countries across the world, people are discriminated on the basis of colour, societal class or financial status. And all; who try to change it; face opposition initially. But, now people have started recognising that this is wrong and the opposition is also not that strong.

Things are changing; but now, we have to hasten this process and make our society strong and successful. It is only when; we are united that we can all be strong.

Student: But, how can I contribute as an individual?

Teacher: By becoming free from fear of good or bad results and expectations of returns for your actions and by not swaying from your duty.

You say; you are small and you can't do it. The young man says, " I have to take care of my career, so I can't do it" and the retired person says, "I have retired now. I will stay away from any duty". If all sections of the society do this, then who is going to contribute?

Staying away from your work or duty is not right; but working without any expectation is the correct way. I will introduce, in a few moments; our guests; who have been working selflessly in our society for many years. They keep the harmony in the country and nobody in the society dares to ask them about their family lineage, instead everyone only recognizes and respects their contribution. Here they are! Please, give them a standing ovation!

Teacher: Please, sirs, take your respective seats and enlighten our children with your presence and experienced words of wisdom.

(All students greet the four guests and sit quietly with a round of applause)

Guest 1 (The Provider): I chose this profession, as I liked to manage, produce and distribute. I handle my accounts; too. I see to it that my farm products reach as many people as possible, with a proper supply chain. My friend manages farm produce to make various items; like cloth, organic fertilizer etc. We are proud members of the business community.

Student: Yes, sir. Thanks to you, we get all the items that we need every day. We understand your contribution is great.

Guest 2 (The Carer): I liked to take care of others, by keeping things in their place and focusing on cleanliness. I clean roads, canals, institutes and homes. My colleagues are working for this purpose and we perform our duties without any discrimination of rich or poor. We are proud members of the community of carers; whose aim is to keep the city and its places clean.

Student: Yes and because of your great contribution, we can move freely in the city and you play an important role in keeping us healthy. Thank you, sir. We are grateful to you and your community of carers.

Teacher: Yes, now; you please introduce yourself, Sir.

Guest 3 (A teacher):

I used to read a lot of books in many fields, like history, geography, physical sciences, biology, social science and had a special interest in the developmental aspects of society; right from the beginning. I used to help my friends in studies. It is my habit and passion to teach as I believe that whatever I know, I must teach others. This is how; I am in this profession.

Student: Thank you, sir. We need teachers in all fields; without whom; the society cannot prosper. Now, I understand that without passing of knowledge; no society can be rich in knowledge. It is this knowledge that teaches us to dare to dream big for bringing transformation. And; so; we are most thankful to your community in all fields. You inspire us for gaining more and more knowledge. Thanks sir for meeting us today.

Teacher: Sir, now, please introduce yourself to our children.

Guest 4 (A soldier): I was always a risk taker. I was a team head of my group in NCC in school. I would always help my neighbours, whenever needed and I was a good scout of my school. This is how; I grew my passion to join the military. I am now a retired captain but my duties towards my nation are still ongoing. With a friend; who is a retired SSP and few other like-minded friends, we have started training camps for house guards. We feel; safety should be the first priority of our town and encourage empower many youngsters to join the police, military and other allied defence services.

Student: Oh, sir! Without you; nothing is safe; in our country. If our town is not safe; we can't be safe. This is; also; very important for every town, city or country. Please, accept our salutes, sir.

Teacher: So, my dear students; what do you feel after hearing these masters of various fields?

Student: Sir, we actually feel enlightened listening to the experienced guests and feel that we have learnt many important things; with which; we can take any type of work happily.

Teacher: Yes, my friends. We are coming close towards the completion of our workshop. All these things, which I shared with you in all these days; is a knowledge that was shared to me by my grandparents. When I received it from them, I experienced that I am free of the ugly discriminative practices and I learnt that all are one. I understood that the service oriented great personalities of our country have come from any and many diverse family backgrounds. All work together for the progress of the society, nation and world at large.

Student: Fantastic sir, we feel free from these ideological bondages and recognize that we must work together with anybody and anyone for the betterment of the society, nation and world at large.

Teacher: That's good. Listen carefully to what am going to tell you. Even though; we see all these four classes as distinct from the outside, do you know all these four classes exist inside every individual?

Student: Oh, we thought all the four are separate from each other. Can you please explain, how the four classes are inside one individual?

Teacher: Yes, I will explain. We all, as individuals, ourselves exercise these four duties in our daily life activities itself.

When you think deep, your mind tells you what is wrong and what is right and during this time, your mind is that of a 'Teacher'. Your hands always guard you from any danger and come forward to save you just like a 'Protector' or guard. Your stomach digests food and your intestine assimilates and distributes all the required mineral and vitamins to all your body parts, thus working as a 'Provider'. And your legs serve you as you travel on all sorts of paths and always assist you wherever you want to go. You can say that they are serving you as a 'Carer'.

Student: Oh ! This is a great perspective. So, how can we discriminate; when we have all four in ourselves?

So, when; we don't follow any discrimination of any sort among people and do our every action; without having any specific expectations, our life will become better and we will be happy in life.

Teacher: Yes. This is all; what we need to go beyond pain and pleasure and experience the bliss of existence. This is the real purpose of human life. All the best to you and your family.

Chapter 18: Points to remember

1. *Understand the four pillars of the society. Know that all are equally essential and never discriminate.*

2. *People are basically of four different temperaments, likings and missions.*

3. *Every individual is born with a purpose. The lineage of an individual has no bearing for an individual; who has realized his/her mission.*

Chapter 19: *Remember all the points you have learnt.*

CHAPTER 19

Nobody can teach anything to anybody

The workshop was complete and the children's regular classes; too; began. But, the students were feeling a little blank; as they had got used to the sessions and were missing them.

The day's first hour was off and so all the students were outside the class. They got together in a huddle and began talking:-

Student 1: I know, yesterday's personality development class was the last one.

Student 2: Yes and I am feeling very empty today.

Student 3: Me too. I want something concrete for me; which I won't forget.

Student 4: Same feeling, my friend. I am wondering, how to take all these teachings that we learnt ahead, without our teacher!

Student 5: Can we bother our sir, once more - for a last message from him to all of us?

Student 6: No yaar. Why trouble him?

Student 7: May be; he will not feel this to be a trouble.

Student 8: Yes, he has always been very friendly with all of us, answering even our silliest of questions.

Student 9: And more over in 1st lesson only, he taught us to not hesitate to ask; if one experienced any difficulty instead of remaining confused.

Student 10: And more over; this would be the last question only.

Student 11: Silence, please. Our sir is approaching towards us.

Student 12: It will be better, if we all ask him together.
(Teacher approaches the students and greets them)

Teacher: Hi, friends! How are you all feeling? All good?

Student 13:   Yes, sir. But, we all need some advice from you. How do we go ahead and face our life's questions, without bothering you more? We just request for one more class.

Student 14:   We want to be here only. We will not bother you to take us out anywhere. Please, sir!

Teacher: No problem. I will only be too happy to comply. Let us all sit down here, below this big peepal tree. I know you are not going to take too much time now as you have understood well all the principles of personality development.

Student: Yes, sir. We only want a few important tips on how we can proceed ahead in life? You have taught us so many important things.

Teacher: I will tell you one more principle. Remember the basic principle -"Nobody can teach anything to anybody"

Student: I am not able to understand, sir. Please explain.

Teacher: See, teachers or masters always teach to all; but only a very few learn. Why? It is because they learn, but teachers get the credit.

Many students are there in class, but only a few pass with flying colours.

Student: Yes, sir. Right!

Teacher: It is so simple. Teacher introduces the concepts to all, but those who learn and follow are the right students, aren't they?

Student: Yes, sir. But, our problem is that; how can we proceed in the absence of a teacher?

Teacher: See, I have explained earlier that, there is a presence of the universal master in the form of the inner spirit within you. If you recognize it and follow the inner instructions, all your problems will be solved.

Student: But, how, sir? What is the way and how can we children understand this? Can you share any example?

Teacher: Yes, there are many and I am sure you; too; have experienced few such moments yourselves.

See, many a times you just open your textbook before exam and read something as per your inner feeling and the same question appears in the paper, isn't it? Have you experienced this? Who suggested you to read that out before the exam.

Student: Yes, sir. I have experienced it and many of my friends; too; have got this experience.

Student: Yes, sir. Once, I changed my road in the last minute and took another route which I never take. But, unexpectedly, I met an old friend who studies in another town on this different route and we both were very happy to see each other, as we met after a very long time. I; still; do not understand, why I took the different route; as I had no specific reason for changing my usual road.

Student: Sir, one day, I was on my way home from school; when I saw a person selling fresh guavas. They looked good and so I bought some. When I came home, I gave it to my mother. She was surprised and happy. And told me that my younger brother was asking for guavas only. She was about to go out and at that same moment, I appeared with the same.

Teacher: So nice to hear. My friends, this presence of mind comes from your inner spirit and is indicatory of the presence of a light that shall always guide and teach you in your life. And, when you become aware of it, you will always receive the guidance and never be alone. So friends, what knowledge was passed on to me, the same, I have passed on to you along with my own experience.

Student: Oh! this is wonderful. Thank you Sir.

Teacher: Recognizing the teacher within your heart and remembering him/her at all times with full faith will always help you and you will remain ever confident to learn more and more.

Student: Yes, sir. Any final permanent guide line, sir?

Teacher: Good question! See we always work individually for individual gains and get a little out of it. But, if you work for yourself; as well as others collectively, the whole world will be benefitted.

Student: How, sir?

Teacher: Think and work for nation building. When you are strong, nation becomes strong and all four pillars become strong. So, always think of the nation. It will give you a vast vision and motivation to work for all to be happy, healthy and prosperous and live a life; where none shall have to experience pain and sorrow.

Student: Thank you, sir. We feel blessed with your last message. This gives us a limitless motivation and we all take a pledge to become worthy citizens of our nation. Please, accept our sincere regards and love forever.

Chapter 19: Points to remember

1. *Teachers teach us. Our duty is to learn.*

2. *Recognize the inner teacher.*

3. *Remember the teachings of the teacher and even in his/her absence, you will feel your teacher's presence.*

4. *One has to grow and contribute in nation building. Working for the betterment of the nation and its peoples can become a source of endless motivation in life.*

5. *Remember all the points you have learnt.*

ABOUT THE AUTHOR

Born in Indore, M.P., on 27th May, 1947; Sri Madhusudan Damle is a teacher and spiritual guide of many experienced teachers, doctors, managers, bankers and professionals in many other disciplines.

In his school; he was the school pupil leader and a champion gymnast who represented M.P. in the nationals. He was; also; an expert in the theatrical arts and a good actor.

He chose to work in the medical profession, first as a representative and later as an executive and gained experience in agriculture, veterinary sciences, allopathy & ayurveda.

In 1982, in Pune; he set up his Ayurvedic distributorship - KVM Enterprises and in 1988, in Pondicherry; he founded KVM Research Laboratories; and researched; developeded many Ayurvedic patent formulations and began exporting them in 1990.

In 2011, he founded Midam Charitable Trust; which has been engaging in various social activities in the fields of children's education through the Krishna's Butter project, therapy for children with special needs through the Vedic Chants Intervention Program (VCIP), women empowerment and more.

In 2022, Damleji wrote this book; inspired from his life experiences, interactions with children of various ages and also his close observation of the educational system over the decades; so that; children can develop a RMA (Right Mental Attitude) and live a happy, healthy and prosperous life.